WILDWOOD FLOWER

DISCARDED
Richmond Public Library

Wildwood Flower is the 1992 Lamont Poetry Selection
of The Academy of American Poets.

From 1954 through 1974 the Lamont Poetry Selection
supported the publication and distribution of a first
collection of poems. Since 1975 this distinguished
award has been given for an American poet's second book.

Judges for 1992: Lucille Clifton, Jorie Graham, and
Robert Morgan.

POEMS BY

Kathryn Stripling Byer

RICHMOND PUBLIC LIBRARY CALIFORNIA

Louisiana State University Press
Baton Rouge and London
1992

Copyright © 1977, 1978, 1979, 1980, 1983, 1984, 1985, 1986, 1987, 1992 by Kathryn Strip-
ling Byer
All rights reserved
Manufactured in the United States of America
First printing
01 00 99 98 97 96 95 94 93 92   5 4 3 2 1

Designer: Amanda McDonald Key
Typeface: Bembo
Typesetter: G&S Typesetters, Inc.
Printer and binder: Thomson–Shore, Inc.

Library of Congress Cataloging-in-Publication Data

Byer, Kathryn Stripling.
    Wildwood flower: poems / by Kathryn Stripling Byer.
        p. cm.
    ISBN 0-8071-1770-6 (cloth). — ISBN 0-8071-1771-4 (paper)
    I. Title.
PS3569.T6965W54   1992
811'.54—dc20   92-2519
                                                           CIP
Grateful acknowledgment is made to the editors of the following publications, in which the
poems noted first appeared: *Appalachian Journal,* "Chestnut Flat Mine," "Croon," "Easter,"
"Soup Pot"; *Arts Journal,* "Bittersweet," "Diamonds," "Lost Soul," "Mary," "Whippoor-
wills," "Wildwood Flower"; *Carolina Quarterly,* "Burning Wing Gap," "Childbirth," "Lul-
laby"; *Georgia Review,* "All Hallows Eve," "Empty Glass," "Sister" (under the title "In-
digo"), "Snowbird"; *Iowa Review,* "Alma," "Extremity"; *Jackson County Poetry Anthology,
1978* (Sylva, N.C.), "Mary Walks in the Fields"; *Nimrod,* "Afterwards, Far from the
Church," "Amazing Grace," "At Kanati Fork," "Black Shawl," "Her Deathbed," "Ivory
Combs," "Midnight," "River Bed," "Trillium"; *Nomad,* "Weep-Willow." "Quilt" was first
published by Firewheel Press Broadsides in 1987. "Ivy, Sing Ivory," "Snow," and "Thaw"
were first published in a chapbook, *Alma,* by Phoenix Press in 1983. "Weep-Willow" also
appeared as the epigraph to *Fair and Tender Ladies,* by Lee Smith (New York, 1988).

The author offers many thanks to Lee Smith, James Applewhite, Fred Chappell, and Pe-
nelope Scambly Schott for their encouragement and advice. "Amazing Grace" is for Gayle
Woody, "Easter" for Willa Mae Pressley, "Ivory Combs" for Linda Mathis, "River Bed"
for Jim Applewhite, and "Weep-Willow" for Lee Smith.

The author also wishes to thank the North Carolina Arts Council and the National Endow-
ment for the Arts for grants that helped provide time and space for the completion of this
book.

Publication of this book has been supported by a grant from the National Endowment for
the Arts in Washington, D.C., a federal agency.

The paper in this book meets the guidelines for permanence and durability of the Committee
on Production Guidelines for Book Longevity of the Council on Library Resources. ∞
```
MAIN
811.54 Byer, Kathryn
Stripling.
     Wildwood flower :



31143004767423              v. 1
```

FOR ISABEL
And in memory of Francis Pledger Hulme

Solitude is deep water . . .
—Emma Bell Miles, *The Spirit of the Mountains*

CONTENTS

Her Deathbed

At Kanati Fork
she was a face fading back into hemlock.
I heard her long skirt rustle,
knowing it sumac and witch-hobble.
She was the wind in my ears,
singing "Sail away, ladies,"
and setting the maple leaves spinning,

a lone woman haunting the trail
till it ended in chimney-stone cast among
wood sorrel. "Who are you?" I asked the shade
where her milk bucket rusted to nothing
but rim. I saw, half-buried
under the leaf mold, a spoon catch the sun.

In her basin
a mirror of water.

Have you entered the storehouses of the snow?
Job 38:22

WILDWOOD FLOWER

I hoe thawed ground
with a vengeance. Winter has left
my house empty of dried beans
and meat. I am hungry

and now that a few buds appear
on the sycamore, I watch the road
winding down this dark mountain
not even the mule can climb
without a struggle. Long daylight

and nobody comes while my husband
traps rabbits, chops firewood, or
walks away into the thicket. Abandoned
to hoot owls and copperheads,

I begin to fear sickness. I wait
for pneumonia and lockjaw. Each month
I brew squaw tea for pain.
In the stream where I scrub my own blood
from rags, I see all things flow
down from me into the valley.

Once I climbed the ridge
to the place where the sky
comes. Beyond me the mountains continued
like God. Is there no place to hide
from His silence? A woman must work

else she thinks too much. I hoe
this earth until I think of nothing
but the beans I will string,
the sweet corn I will grind into meal.

We must eat. I will learn
to be grateful for whatever comes to me.

EMPTY GLASS

Last night I stood ringing
my empty glass under
the black empty sky and beginning, of all

things, to sing.
The mountains paid no attention.
The cruel ice did not melt.
But just for a moment the hoot owl grew silent.
And somewhere the wolves hiding out
in their dens opened cold, sober eyes.

Here's to you
I sang, meaning
the midnight
the dark moon
the empty well,

meaning myself
upon whom the snow fell
without any apology.

SOUP POT

I stir it and think
of the garden plowed under,
the rats in the barn gnawing
all I have harvested,

what I must do
every day, boil this bone
until nothing is left,
neither marrow nor
sinew, and supper is water
I've hauled up the hillside,
a little salt added for flavor,
a little dried parsley.

This is the year the worst happens.
How well I have learned to imagine it,
as if already my hands twist the goat's empty teat
or reach down into dust at the bottom of sacks.
Let the men argue what bark
grown thick as an axe handle prophesies.
I have my own thoughts,
these meat scraps and bone chips.

I stir them
and stir them.

ALMA

Two dead leaves
on the table and ice

floats on milk like the ashes
of leaves. Oak
twigs kindle
and fire leaps like a prayer, "Give us

breath." When I open
the door and breathe deeply
the cold air inflames me.
The fire seizes log after log.

In the garden my husband burns
dead stalks of squash and potatoes.
I sweep my dust into the coals
and our smoke mingles over the orchard.

In autumn I sweep the floor gladly.
I gather the crumbs from the cupboard,
and the rinds of the apples.
When my dustbin grows heavy,
I give what it holds to the fire
and the fire sings its song:

raise your dead
from the earth, make a fire
of their bones,
set them free

to be sky,
to be nothing at all.

BURNING WING GAP

Not among the soaring
hawk nor yet among the wild

boar rooting into black
earth, but outside my kitchen

door it turns to crimson
as if we'd brought back the fire

we first found on our courting
trail and kept it burning

by the clothesline where his socks
drip and the gray sleeves

of my linsey dress. He'll say
the leaves are not the same,

more heart-shaped, golden
flamed. A dogwood,

after all. But what do I care
for the difference in a leaf?

I want him to come here
and say for once that he remembers

when I led him up the darkest
side of Snowbird like a blind man

through those bushes burning to the edge
of where we stopped and sky began.

ALL HALLOWS EVE

I go by taper of cornstalk,
the last light of fields wreathed in woodsmoke,
to count the hens left in the chickenhouse
raided by wild dogs and foxes.
Our rooster crows far up the hillside
where three piles of rocks mark the graves
of nobody I ever knew.
Let their ghosts eat him!
Each year they grow hungrier,
wanting the squash run to seed in our garden,
the tough spikes of okra. Tonight while the moon
lays her face on the river and begs
for a love song, they'll come down the mountain
to steal the last apples I've gathered.

They'll stand at the window and ask us
for whom is that buttermilk set on the table?
That platter of cold beans?
They know we will pay them no heed.
It's the wind, we will say,
watching smoke sidle out of the fireplace,
or hearing the cellar door rattle.

No wonder they go away
always complaining how little the living
have learned, on our knees
every night asking God for a clean heart,
a pure spirit. Spirit? They kick
up the leaves round the silent house.
What good is spirit without hands for walnut
to stain, without ears for the river
to fill up with promises? What good,
they whisper, returning to nothing, what good
without tongue to cry out to the moon,
"Thou hast ravished my heart, O my sister!"

MIDNIGHT

You no longer sing
in the darkness, "My lady love
sleeps in a hazel green
bower." Those nights
by the glow of the lamp
I lay waiting for you
to come back from the spring
house and say, "Hear
that whippoorwill singing
its heart away?" I should
have wrapped you in words
like a soft blanket.
Why did I say nothing
I might remember tonight
as we lie here not speaking
of where you will go
in the morning? Not even
you slept when we first lay
together so quietly, what
was it we heard like the river
that carries the moonlight
away from this valley
you said was our Heaven?
"The wind," you say,
turning away to the wall.
"It was only the wind passing."

CROON

Like your letters I open and close every evening,
this dead garden ought to be burned before
snow settles over the Balsams. What news
but the creaking of cold branches,

bone in the dog's teeth or rope
on the gallows' wood? You hitched your wagon
and rode away calling, "Don't open
your door to a stranger." Ha,

rabbits out late for what's left
of summer, a rifle's cocked
somewhere, a pot hanging empty!
When snakes burrow into the frozen

grass, I dig my coat
from the trunk like a second skin.
Where are you now that the door's
locked and there is no quilt

on your bed? When the moon
is so big I can't sleep I say this
is the same moon you see in Kentucky
or Tennessee. Even the wind

comes from some place where
maybe you are, writing, "Wait
for me." Where would I go?
And with whom? Darling, hear

me. I sing
like the owl.
Shularoon.
Shularoon.

SNOWBIRD

At midday you steadied our boat on the riverbank,
pointing your rifle to some snowy height.
"I will build you a house there," you promised.
I thought I saw sun on my windows,
the flash of a silver bird's wing. Can a bird
sing like ice melting? I never heard him.

Perhaps even now in the darkness he glows
like the lamp I left burning
the night your bay mare wandered
up the hill, dragging your saddle.

Sometimes he flies over me scrubbing
the hearthstone or threading my loom with the drabbest
of homespun. I never look up
into sky when I walk through the woods

for it's ginseng and bloodroot
a woman must take home, not feathers
to melt in her hands, little more
than the sweat after labor.

Someday I will not think again about lace
on the cuffs of a blouse
or the earrings you fondled with cold fingers.
I will forget water
under our boat, how the rocks sang
like birds heading south.

THAW

Hauling my buckets
up this trail, my heavy
boots sliding on ice,
I have moved as a mule

moves, without joy,
and wondered what mules think
when they drag a wagon home.
We found ours frozen

to death in the pasture and what
did he think as his haunches grew stiff,
empty belly stopped rumbling? I thought
how I too might have simply stood

still and become ice, I was that
tired of lifting cold water.
Today the road's shedding
its ice like a snakeskin,

like my own calloused skin
I will scour this very night,
though the almanac says spring
is six weeks away. It lies,

surely it lies. Such a winter
demands early spring, for my face
is so sad from desiring the sun
and my hair dull as rope in the barn.

I am tired of the sight of me
frozen in glass every morning,
as if the moon waited for stones
I will throw in the water.

EXTREMITY

Pity my cold feet in bed.
The doctor says I need warm blood
down there, gives me a tonic
that burns in my gut
not my feet. My toes curl
in the blankets like French knots
I used to pull so tight

the thread broke. My fingers dig
into my stomach. Small wonder
my dreams are of frostbite,
my toes dropping off like ruined berries,
my fingers strewn over the snow.

When I wake I work hard until noon.
I collect every nail paring,
skin faint as snow on the pumice stone.
Even the hair woven into my comb
I can spin into strong, silver thread,
and I gather the stubs
of the candles from every long evening
like eggs in my apron. A cup of tea

and I sit down to sew
nothing. I watch the gray sky
through the eye of each needle
my fingers have ever held up to the light
and I wait for the mousetrap to spring

in the pantry where peaches still cling
to their stones. I have made my house ready
for ice. Every hole's stuffed
with cloth. Every window's nailed shut.
When the sun sets I turn the key
twice in the lock, blow

the candles out. Nothing can come
to me now. I have no blessings to count.

I count my cold fingers and toes.

LULLABY

Snow is lying on my roof.
I cannot breathe.
Two tons of snow lie on my roof

heavy as the sea,
the loft of grain,
the desert as it gathers sand,
and I have only two small flames
beside my bed. I hear the sea

when I lie down, the sea
inside my head.
The candles sputter when the wind blows.
Snow falls from the trees

like sacks of grain.
No seed can root in snow.
It cannot breathe.
My roof is like an unplowed field.

Who walks upon it?
Rafters creak
as if a wishbone cracked
and I had wished the sky to fall.

LOST SOUL

Wind shakes the latch on my door
as if someone is knocking.
I stand at the sink, my hands cold

from the clothes I have washed.
On the line they are tossed like lost souls,
and when wind shakes the latch on my door

like a summons, I shut my eyes.
Nightgowns float over the toolshed.
I stand at the sink, my hands cold

and do not fetch them home.
I know better than walk down this mountain
when wind shakes the latch on my door

as if someone is knocking indeed.
Against solitude I have no aid.
Must I stand at the sink, my hands cold

when I might strike a match to dry kindling?
The shape of my kettle's a comfort
when wind shakes the latch on my door.
Yet I stand at the sink, my hands cold.

QUILT

What I see out the door
is a tree trunk
my arms cannot span
and a trough where the mule drinks.

I see many birds eat the crusts
I have scattered.
I see their wings shiver
like eyelids. I see the trail

disappear downhill,
no sign of you on it,
your dust rising toward me,
the flash of your bridle.

I see my front yard as a jumble
of shapes I have never succeeded in piecing
together. The empty pail. Tracks
over new snow. The rats in the woodpile.

What else can I call it
but *Waiting for Spring?*
That old patchwork. The dead
sleep beneath it forever.

I went down . . . to look at the blossoms of the valley.

Song of Sol. 6:11

Come down
to bloodroot that blooms
for a day only under the hemlock,

the wind dawdles
all afternoon while I worry
the witch-bridles out of my hair

with a comb that lacks most
of its ebony teeth. *Straw,*
I hear Sister whisper, *the color*

of straw left to rot
in the fields. On the porch rail
my crazy quilts flap their calico

wings as if waking themselves
from my long winter's bad dream of nothing
but bones underneath this white

shimmy the wind whips and raises.
I throw down my broken comb,
shake my hair so hard the sky spins

one sun-gilded strand slowly
into the weeds. As I lower my head
to the basin of rainwater, I see

her, She of the Squaw Eyes
that never blink. Oh, for a blooming
cheek. Dimpled chin. Kiss

me, I tease the longsuffering
lips coming closer
as if to ask *Who is this?*

Fool, I say,
see for yourself.
And I laugh in the water's face.

TRILLIUM

April, and I have come far as the trail's
fork to whisper it, watery sound
like the swollen creek running beside us
the morning we left church and walked till

he threw down his coat on the grass.
How the ridges were rife with this word's blooming
multitudes, sprung out of nothing
and overnight, as if the souls of all creatures

with wings buried under the leaf mold had risen
and, but for our presence, might take to the sky
singing praise! Nothing moved.
Neither wind, nor the scurry of mice

in the underbrush. Far away I heard the bluejays
rejoicing. And then his breath filling my ear
with my name. Soul of Sweet Mercy,
I should have covered my head with my shawl

and kept silent! Though we spoke of love,
I know now it means little
but loneliness. Better if he had said, "Trillium,
trillium!" I might have known what

he meant: Flood tide.
Both of us well-nigh to drowning.

IVORY COMBS

He sat on the porch every morning
and dreamed he would someday go wandering farther
than all he could see beyond Burning Wing Gap.
"Hear the wind," he sighed.
"Just like a woman she never stops calling me."

"What does she say?" I teased.
"That you're a cold-hearted man who cares more
for his rambling than for any wife?"

How he laughed!
Then he straightened his hat
and tried hard to look solemn.
"That song you sing when you turn sad,
Oh, it's down, down went her ivory combs,
sing it now," he said,
pulling me onto his lap.

I untangled his hands from my waist
and stood up again, smoothing my apron,
for I had grown tired of the old songs,
their garlands of rue and their thorny vines.
So many winding sheets.

I walked away to the edge of the apple trees,
watching him over my shoulder.
I let down my hair,
and he took off his hat,
tossed it far as he could in the sunlight.
The shady grass lay like a promise between us,
concealing the first of its gay wings
and meadow-sweet. "Gypsy girl,"
I heard him calling.
I watched him come after me,
crushing the wildflowers under his feet.

CHRISTMAS

1 ✸ Mary

Sometimes in bed he would lay his big hand
on my womb and say tenderly, "Gabriel,"
for he would have his child bearing God's
message. Not once did he think of the one
to whom God sent his angel,
the girl crouching under the olive trees,
letting the flax she was spinning fall
into the sand. All that autumn
I thought of her sweeping the floor
of her father's house. I heard the gossip
behind her as she bore the water jugs
home from the well, spilling nary a drop
though her knees trembled. I came to know
how the hair fell away from the nape
of her neck as she bent over stitches
so tiny no seam would press into His body.
By Christmas Eve I understood how she sat
on the donkey, one hand resting over her womb
and the other behind her. I knew how
her back ached the long ride to Bethlehem.
That night I dreamt of the cold stable earth
that she lay upon, asking for water,
for light, for the song of the angels
she knew must be hovering. "Mary," I cried,
for I knew she was shivering next to the sheep.
How I wished that the lambs might go to her
and nuzzle her fingertips! "Mary,
my Mary," I whispered, and stroked
through my own flesh the flesh of my child.

2 ❦ Mary Walks in the Fields

Full of her child's grace, she walks
down the unyielding furrows, her body rejoicing
in Him as a strong basket bears forth its grain
to the threshing floor. Loudly she sings
of the one she holds safe in her womb
while she strides through the noisy wind,
paying no heed to the small branches laden
with ice, or the thorns clinging fast to the hem
of her skirt. Rising over the mountains
the full moon moves quickly, the month almost
gone when too soon she must labor Him
onto the cold earth from which, in the fullness
of time, He will bid the fruit come
and the honeybees swarm to the work of His Father,
for it has been prophesied. What can she
do but keep singing as she would have Him sing
when he walks from one dusty town to another?

3 ❧ Whippoorwills

At midnight I went to the stable
to see if the cattle knelt, knowing he laughed
at my foolishness. Once as a boy
he had done the same, dazed by the stories
of oxen that fell to their knees on this night.
There'd been nothing to see, he said,
nothing but fox tracks he followed
so far in the woods he had cried out
for help. "I am going," I vowed

and set out with my lantern through snow
that clung fast to my bare head,
my shawl. "Like a mother's hair
swaddling her darling," I crooned to the baby
who kicked in my womb. I no longer feared
falling upon the steep pathway that led
to the stable where each of the beasts
watched me enter. A cow mooed.

I sat on a bucket to rest. Like a child
I was full of what waited for me
in the morning, the fat orange and
peppermint stick. I was happy. What was it
my grandmother sang to us? "Cold on His cradle
the dewdrops are shining." She promised me
wonders if I'd but believe them, the elderbush
blooming in snow, and at daybreak
a barn full of whippoorwills singing.

4 ❧ Snow

Early I walk through plentiful leaves
and see on the far ridges snow gleaming
like a mirage. So the memory of waking to such
a great fire in our hearth as the Holy Child
would have been proud to feel warming His blessed feet,
and again through the ice on our windows the day
of His birth flaring over the summit of Windy Roost:
can I believe in it? "Snowbird," I whisper
and wait for the wings of the sun to pass over the trail

I climb, dreaming of snow. How I long to sleep
under it, as if I never must wake before dawn
and go down to the cowstall and spring, dragging back
on my skirt a white hem I wring over the basin;
as if beneath heavy boots snow never hardens
to ice on which I fear a woman's bones break
like her baby's new toys. Though I lay me down

under the whitest of linen around which the lace
hides like wood sorrel, how shall I sleep
unless I conjure under a rising moon snow
like the light in the darkness the preacher says
faith is, like cities I hear tell of waiting
beyond the last mountain, where lamps
burn all night in the dirty streets?

CHILDBIRTH

Someday I will tell her the fire roared
for what seemed like days and the rooster crowed
so loud I ordered the midwife to fetch the axe
under my bed. There was yellow brush
far up the mountain I watched
until night came. And blood.

I remember that. No thaw
will ever make me so afraid as I was
of that flood taking six sheets
to stanch, that still stains like a birthmark
the one I would not let them burn.

It was March. I remember her cries
like a pumphandle braying. I walked against
everyone's wishes outside to the spring
where the milk jars sat, chastened
to such irreproachable sweetness
I knelt and drank gallons of sunlight.

BITTERSWEET

Under the thin flannel nightgown,
my daughter's ribs: frail
harp I stroke
as if I might make some lovely sound
of those bones. At my breast

she would cling to the nipple,
my milk like a sudden thaw straining
the downspout let down, oh
the stony earth blossomed, I saw
my pots brimming, my skirts full
of apples. I rocked her to sleep
singing, "Little bird,
little bird under my wing." Hear

my voice crack! I cough
and keep silent. Now she is the one
in this house who sings, crooning
like wind in the chimney. My sweet songs
have all blown away,
one by one, down the mountain.

LINEAGE

This red hair
I braid while she
sits by the cookstove
amazes her. Where
did she get hair the color
of wildfire, she wants to know,
pulling at strands of it
tangled in boar-bristles.
I say from Sister, God knows
where she is, and before
her my grandmother you
can't remember because
she was dead by the time
you were born, though you hear
her whenever I sing,
every song handed down
from those sleepless nights
she liked to sing through
till she had no time
left for lying awake
in the darkness and talking
to none save herself.
And yet, that night
I sat at her deathbed
expecting pure silence,
she talked until dawn
when at last her voice
failed her. She thumbed out
the candle between us
and lifted her hand
to her hair as if what
blazed a lifetime might still
burn her fingers. Yes,
I keep a cinder of it

in my locket I'll show you
as soon as I'm done telling
how she brought up from
the deep of her bedclothes
that hairbrush you're holding
and whispered, "You
might as well take it."

HER DEATHBED

1 ♣ Banshee

Tonight? Yes, tonight. Hurry,
lock the gate, flog the mule into the stable
and tie down the haystacks. That wind,
hear it? What comes on such wind you know
very well, how the sly little moans will grow
quickly to mother's wails, all the ways
children can die, rusty nails, broken
slats over swollen creeks, clogged throats
and burning wounds. Don't listen.
Fire up your hearth. Fill your tea kettle.
Hammer your walnuts against a flat stone.
Stomp your buck and wing dance
so the coffee cups rattle and if nothing else
works, why then you must sing your hey
diddle-dum-doh, what the farmer's old woman
sang, tweaking the devil's cold nose
till the sun rises, all of us safe
for a little while longer, though nobody knows
for how long. There will always be
snakes in the woodpile
and men casting dice for a woman's soul.
Mind me, don't laugh,
and don't linger too long at the window
that ought to stay closed.
If you hear a scythe whisper not far
from your neck, don't look out.
All the beautiful cornstalks will fall.

2 ♣ Solitaire

she said and pulled out
the deck of cards last time
we came calling. Red hearts
laid down on the bedspread

and black bruises under
the dirty sheets. "You needn't stay,"
said the last man to bring her black coffee
in bed. "As if we were not kinswomen,"

I heard my mother complain, climbing
back into the buckboard. Four miles without words,
though I wanted to scream at the stupid mules
pointed toward home with no questions asked.

Had they been lies, all those stories
I'd heard round the table? How she sang *Lorena*
on any front porch while the old women wept
in their aprons. How she traveled

twenty years, train tickets filling her pockets
like dollar bills, somebody waiting at every stop,
somebody handsome with small gifts.
A silk ribbon.

Rose petals.
Ruby that quickened in three claws of gold
when she held out her hand
to me, wanting a kiss. It would be mine,

she promised, for I was her namesake.
Her singing dove. Grandmother,
that ring you wore till we covered your head
with a clean sheet and sat down to wait for your coffin,

I lost it feeding the pigs.
And now where is it? Buried in mud?
Or still waiting for me in a sow's carcass,
cold as a drop of your blood?

3 ❧ Hawk

Up here I am safe.
There's no need they should come.
Let them sweat at their stoves,
stirring mayhaws until the juice spins
a red thread. Let them cherish the jars
on their shelves. I was never their fool.
Rainbows end in the mud where
I come from. No wind, and the clouds
stay so long they grow yellow
as old satin curtains nobody can open
or wants to, for nothing is out there
but windmills that won't move
or corn that won't grow. It's no good
for a woman. That stillness.
How long have I been gone? A hundred
years? Grandmother prayed I'd come
home and my mother said I'd live
to curse my contrariness. Ha,
I curse women who won't live
to hear the wind blow all night long
as it does over Cherokee Gap. I will
never go back. Can't they understand that?
I do not want their peach wine,
their jelly too thick to be spooned.
God forbid I should ever eat fruitcake again!
Here they come up that road like a caravan
out of the flatlands, with tears
in their eyes and their lips puckered
round their sweet words. But I swear
by that hawk I see biding its time
over Warwoman Ridge I will not iron

my black dress and wear my hair tight
in a bun. I will not throw the first clod
of dirt in the hole. Lock the door,
girl, and tell them there's nobody home.

At night she watched the road
and sang. I'd sigh and settle on the floor
beside her. One song led
to one more song. Some unquiet grave.
A bed of stone. The ship that spun round
three times 'ere it sank,
near ninety verses full of grief.
She sang sad all night long

and smiled, as if she dared me
shed a tear. Sweet Lizzie Creek swung low
along the rocks, and dried beans rattled
in the wind. Sometimes her black dog howled
at fox or bear, but she'd not stop,
no, not for God Himself, not even if He came
astride a fine white horse and bore the Crown
of Glory in His hands. The dark was all
she had. And sometimes moonlight
on the ceaseless water. "Fill my cup,"

she'd say, and sip May moonshine
till her voice came back as strong as bullfrogs
in the sally grass. You whippoorwills
keep silent, and you lonesome owls go haunt
another woman's darkest hours. Clear,

clear back I hear her singing me to sleep.
"Come down," she trolls,
"Come down among the willow
shade and weep, you fair
and tender ladies left to lie alone,
the sheets so cold,
the nights so long."

SISTER

That morning we sat on the porch
while you wove what you whispered was cloth
for your marriage bed, blue for his eyes,
his undying devotion, you sang softly
over the thump of the batten, "Come go

with me, my pretty little miss,
come go with me, my lady." Your hair
was too long, I thought, coiled way too high,
and the color you wove much too blue
for a good woman's coverlid. As if you

knew what I thought, you leaned over
and hissed, "He's a tall man with black hair
and only the littlest of stubble around
his mouth." I felt my cheeks burn while you
laughed so gaily the combs in your hair fell

about us! I busied myself with the fleece
in my lap, as I do now, for though
you are many years gone, I still envy
you, tossing your hair in the sun
and believing he'd love you forever.

INDIGO

The last thing you did
before you disappeared was cut
warp threads and leave me
to gather the handful

of blue yarn scraps
next morning. Then you were
over and done with.
Not even a note,

though we looked on the floor.
In the grass. Called your name
down the trace. You had taken
some two-day-old cornbread

and left the back door
open. I was so young
I believed you had galloped
away into that gypsy's

ballad you must have been
singing, your last
weaving flung like a lie
round your shoulders.

CHESTNUT FLAT MINE

They say the fringe of her shawl clung
like lichen to creek rock
and under the laurel her sash looked
for all the sad world like a garter snake.

Farther on something so sheer
it was almost invisible floated away
on the Toe River. Red
said the woman who watched it go by,

baby-blue said her little girl stoning
the water with acorns. (Did he stroke
her silken leg after he'd unlaced
her tiny black shoe? Did he say Little

Darling, you're mine and what good
are your fancy ways now?) God Almighty,
they say they heard screams floating
down, light as what I imagine a town woman

wears underneath all her finery,
but when they came to the old mine by late
afternoon, they found only her gloves
thrown aside in the larkspur. Her dress

was laid out like a corpse with a rose
in its lap, on its lily-white bosom
a bird's nest of wrinkles as if a man's
head had lain ever so gently there.

around me,
unraveling its garland
of snakeroot
and cobweb, her
black thoughts made
manifest night
after night as she
labored, her silver
hook gleaming by
candlelight. Memory
chained unto
memory: hawk
sailing, smoke curling
out of the burned
fields, her name
written fancy in black
ink, the words
in her letter, the two
words, *Remember
me*. Nights I can't
sleep I hear
wind shove the dead
leaves along like my own
thoughts, those rag
taggle gypsies she sang
about, all of them black
shawled and stealing
away to their dirty
work, digging as
always past earthworm
and ground water,
tremor of mine
shaft where rocks bear
the imprint of ancient

anemone. They bring
her back piece by
piece to me, even the sound
of her breath in my
oldest dream. "What
will you make
of this?" they whisper,
filling my arms
with a snatch of her
hair, muddy ribbons, this
tangle of black roots
that drags my hands down.

COBWEBS

From the table where
I sit dressed up
for church, my bonnet
pulled down to my
eyebrows and my dinner
basket proper on my knees,
I frown against the sun
that, free of clouds
a moment, makes the cobwebs
strung between my
porch rails shimmer.
Signs! God's signs
hide everywhere like
hooks. Like trap
lines in the current
snaring some bright
pattern I can't see
for looking out the wrong
way or not looking
while I sit here,
scrubbed and corseted
for Easter's singing
of the old Arise
and See His Glory
climbing up the hills
of morning like these
cobwebs sun might turn
to Jacob's Ladders
if I let it through
my squinted eyes.

EASTER

Where my father's house stood
at the edge of the cove is a brown church
the faithful call Bosom of God.
I have come back to sit at the window
where I can see apple trees bud
while the preacher shouts death has no victory.

Everywhere dogwoods are blooming
like white flesh this man claims
is devil's work: woman who tasted
the apple and disobeyed God. But for Christ
we are doomed to the worms waking under
these hills I would rather be climbing

again with my father's goats bleating
so loud I can't hear this man say
I must ask the Lord pardon for what
I've come back to remember—the sun
on my neck as I shook loose my braids
and bent over the washpot. My bare feet

were frisky. If wind made the overalls
dance on the clothesline, then why
shouldn't I? Who's to tell
me I should not have shouted for joy
on this hill? It's the wind I praise God for
today, how it lifted my hair like a veil.

AMAZING GRACE

That sure-as-God white
paint that blinds when the sun
glances off it at noon

moves the preacher to say "Peace
go with you," and send us forth
into the grass with our baskets

and tablecloths we spread like islands
of plenitude. Now let us gather among the graves
leading like stepping-stones down

to the meadow where deer
come to feed in the shadow of Ancient
of Days. There the thunder

lives, God's voice,
the old prophets threaten, but why
should He speak to us only in anger?

That playing of wind
in the witch-hobble could be His drawing
nigh. Could be He's singing

like bees on the applecake,
soothing the children to sleep
while their mothers fall silent,

remembering winter nights'
watch over sickbeds and small coffins
sealed against morning

light. "Wake up!"
their fathers call, hitching the wagons
and sounding each living

name: Willa Mae.
Almarine. Emma Bell. One
by one rising and

rubbing their eyes, they
see white paint and everywhere
dogwood white flame.

AFTERWARDS, FAR FROM THE CHURCH

bells, my way back through balsam
seems darker than when I set out
for the grassy cove. Sundays a storm
always threatens by afternoon,
woods full of churchgoers singing
their leave-taking, *Over, our meeting
is over,* as I urge the mule to climb

faster, lest I hear you years ago
shuffle your feet at my side, meaning *Come
with me.* Almost your wife, who's to care,
I thought, turning to you at the last
chorus, hands all around us clasped tight
against parting. As we rode toward
Mossy Creek, I could hear voices still

singing, as now, when it seems many miles
till the women no longer wail mournfully
over the men's droning: *Save us!*
The Promised Land they yearn to see,
not an earthly creek, late-blooming columbine,
bed of wet maple leaves we made
beyond any singing but that of the ravens.

DIAMONDS

This, he said, giving the hickory leaf
to me. *Because I am poor.*
And he lifted my hand to his lips,
kissed the fingers that might have worn
gold rings if he had inherited

bottomland, not this
impossible rock where the eagles soared
after the long rains were over. He stood
in the wet grass, his open hands empty,
his pockets turned inside out.

Queen of the Meadow, he teased me
and bowed like a gentleman.
I licked the diamonds off the green
tongue of the leaf, wanting only
that he fill his hands with my hair.

IVY, SING IVORY

1

Like women, the dogwoods go nowhere
and wait for their season, the sun coming back
like a sea-roving laddie. By May Day
the ground will be white with their fare-thee-wells
no man will heed, his boots grinding
a path through the leaf mold. Such pretty things,
Mama said, touching the ivory lace
of my wedding clothes. What good are they
to me now? Every night I see stars falling,
white petals into the wilderness.

2

The church bell rings Easter
all morning like, clear-broken, ice
and beneath it the almost unmoving water.

3

White water charges the banks
after rain has been heavy.
I hear it wherever I go,
like the swirl of my dress
as I stand up suddenly,
kicking the chair from my path.

4

Leaves rasp underfoot half-a-day's
climb to the summit. A possum sways
four branches heavenward.
Silver bells,
what sweeter music
than silence? The snail travels

slowly toward water that's been gone
for centuries, rocked by the tidesong
of wind sweeping leaves back
and forth through the gap.

5

Down to the gristmill I follow the creek swollen
so loud by rain I can't hear myself
sing ho-a-honey-ho. Lady Luck's
left me a buckeye to warm
in my pocket all day like an earring
the old woman pulled from her dirty pack
whispering, "Filigree."
"Gypsies," my Mama said,
pointing me back to the crochet hook
stuck in a tangle of tiny white stitches.
"It's too hard," I cried, throwing down
all my fancywork. Fast as I could
I set out for the top of Bald Ridge,
asking why can't I keep walking out of this
endless blue sky into somebody else's
life, fiddles and red skirt
that tickles the floorboards till
dawn. But I knew I could never go far
from the sound of this creek tumbling down
to the lilies of Cullowhee Valley
that bloom like a garland of lace
on my doorsill. Oh ivy, sing ivory,
rosebud and thorn! If only this afternoon
really were endless alongside the gay Tuckasegee
where now I ask, watching its broken light leaving
me, why can't this water run smooth as stone?

RIVER BED

And so I lie down
and let water throw quilt after
quilt on me, each of them older than any I know
how to piece and called endless
names none of us knows how to utter,
beginning with rain wearing down the gray rock
of these mountains where all night the wind
among sycamores scatters dry leaves like a lifetime
of scraps from an old woman's sewing box.
They cling to current like calico Hands
All Around or a True Lover's Knot
flowing downhill forever.
The trout enters this one,
and kingfisher snips golden thread
from the selvage of that one. A thousand,

thousand cater-cornered remnants
of dawn dally over me. Crazy quilt up to my chin
in this morning, I settle my body in silt
like a snake shedding, season by season, its stocking
of skin. Surely nobody knows where to find me
but you, though by now you've forgotten
my promise to sail away someday
on sunlight, your promise to follow me
far as the ocean itself. What you followed was sky
standing open through chestnut and beech as you rode
away, leaving me nothing but time
to remember you, day unto
day stitched, the thread knotted. Let me cut free
all my memories, each one a Heart's
Seal of light on the surface! If you should come home
from your long journey, calling me
far down the valley, my name on your lips close

to singing, I'll shiver
and hide myself under the laurel leaves.
Step from the thicket
and whistle, I'll run away into the green
silence, into the empty air. Lose
you. But Love, look around. See that
lone strand of silver hair carried downriver?